MIX
Papier aus verantwortungsvollen Quellen
Paper from responsible sources
FSC® C105338

Alena Eikens

Changing readers' attitudes?

The representation of discrimination in the Harry Potter novels

Anchor Academic
Publishing

Eikens, Alena: Changing readers' attitudes? The representation of discrimination in the Harry Potter novels, Hamburg, Anchor Academic Publishing 2017

Buch-ISBN: 978-3-96067-164-0
PDF-eBook-ISBN: 978-3-96067-664-5
Druck/Herstellung: Anchor Academic Publishing, Hamburg, 2017

Bibliografische Information der Deutschen Nationalbibliothek:
Die Deutsche Nationalbibliothek verzeichnet diese Publikation in der Deutschen Nationalbibliografie; detaillierte bibliografische Daten sind im Internet über http://dnb.d-nb.de abrufbar.

Bibliographical Information of the German National Library:
The German National Library lists this publication in the German National Bibliography. Detailed bibliographic data can be found at: http://dnb.d-nb.de

All rights reserved. This publication may not be reproduced, stored in a retrieval system or transmitted, in any form or by any means, electronic, mechanical, photocopying, recording or otherwise, without the prior permission of the publishers.

Das Werk einschließlich aller seiner Teile ist urheberrechtlich geschützt. Jede Verwertung außerhalb der Grenzen des Urheberrechtsgesetzes ist ohne Zustimmung des Verlages unzulässig und strafbar. Dies gilt insbesondere für Vervielfältigungen, Übersetzungen, Mikroverfilmungen und die Einspeicherung und Bearbeitung in elektronischen Systemen.

Die Wiedergabe von Gebrauchsnamen, Handelsnamen, Warenbezeichnungen usw. in diesem Werk berechtigt auch ohne besondere Kennzeichnung nicht zu der Annahme, dass solche Namen im Sinne der Warenzeichen- und Markenschutz-Gesetzgebung als frei zu betrachten wären und daher von jedermann benutzt werden dürften.

Die Informationen in diesem Werk wurden mit Sorgfalt erarbeitet. Dennoch können Fehler nicht vollständig ausgeschlossen werden und die Diplomica Verlag GmbH, die Autoren oder Übersetzer übernehmen keine juristische Verantwortung oder irgendeine Haftung für evtl. verbliebene fehlerhafte Angaben und deren Folgen.

Alle Rechte vorbehalten

© Anchor Academic Publishing, Imprint der Diplomica Verlag GmbH
Hermannstal 119k, 22119 Hamburg
http://www.diplomica-verlag.de, Hamburg 2017
Printed in Germany

Content

Introduction..1
1. Discrimination: The fear of the Other?..2
    1.1 Racism: Culture as marker for difference..4
    1.2 Slavery: The (ongoing) oppression of blacks..6
    1.3 Ill and Disabled: A burden for society?...7
2 Harry Potter – A short introduction...9
    2.1 The importance of blood-status: Are magical children of non-magical parents
        inferior witches and wizards?..10
    2.2 Unpaid work and abuse: House-elves in Harry Potter...................................14
    2.3 Non-magical children and Werewolves in the wizarding world....................18
3 *"The greatest magic of* Harry Potter"..20
4 Reader identification..21
Conclusion..25
Literature..28

Introduction

When Joanne K. Rowling published her first *Harry Potter* novel in 1997, probably nobody expected the tremendous success her writing debut was going to bring her. By 2013, around 450 million books have been sold, and the series has been translated into 73 different languages (cf. TIME 2013). The huge popularity of the seven-book series led not only to an equally successful series of film adaptations, but also to a variety of well selling merchandise. Children and adults alike are enchanted by the wizarding world that Rowling so meticulously created.

However, although several scholars dealt with *Harry Potter* on a scientific level, there are also still those who deride them. The books are said to be too childish, of too little literary value to deal with them on a serious level (cf. Patterson 2009, vii). Yet, a close look at the topics shows a wide range worthy of discussion. Rowling uses her fantasy world as a metaphor for our own world, depicting rights and wrongs in many different fields. One of the main themes is even a very controversial one: discrimination. Moreover, "[by] creating fictional racial 'others', author J.K. Rowling has essentially replicated a great deal of the world's history of racism – from racist ideology, to slavery [...]" (Molle 2013, 2). However, Rowling did not just invent a world in black and white, nor does she "simply tell her readership that prejudice and discrimination are social ills" (Brown 2008, 9). Rather, she created a world for the readers to explore and find things out for themselves as the story continued.

In this paper, I claim that the representation of discrimination in the *Harry Potter* series influences the readers in a positive way and that they are likely less prejudiced against stigmatised groups after reading the books. Although there are many characters who are not entirely good or entirely bad, the overall message seems to be that good people accept others regardless of their status, while the villains are those who oppress them. I claim that this depiction has a long-term effect on the reader.

Even today, discrimination is still a topic that we encounter on a near-daily basis. Although there are many organisations fighting for equal rights for all people, still many others have a discriminatory mindset. Hence, it is important to find ways to moderate potential prejudiced behaviour. To wrap this possible effect in a story that compels people of all ages, from very young children to adults, is a valid way to raise awareness.

In chapter 1, I will give a short introduction to the mechanisms of discrimination and how they come to be. I will then deal with three specific forms of discrimination. The first – racism – is a very wide topic for which I will give a definition and short history before explaining forms and displays of modern racism. Following that, I will give an overview of slavery and its impact on black people in our time. Strictly speaking, slavery is a form of racism, but I will deal with this particular aspect in an extra chapter because Rowling has a different metaphor for slavery in her books, as we will later see. The last type of discrimination will be that of ill and disabled people.

Chapter 2 will start with a short introduction to the *Harry Potter* series and an analysis of its narration as well as its effect on the reader. The chapter will continue with the implementation of the aforementioned ways of discrimination. Many wizards in Rowling's fictional world judge others based on their blood status, that is, whether their ancestors have been wizards as well. How this metaphor of racism is expressed on both the side of the good wizards as well as that of the villains will be analysed in this chapter. The house-elves, on the other hand, provide a good image of slavery, as they are employed without payment and generally treated very poorly. The depiction of illness and disability finds expression in the introduction of werewolves and Squibs, children of wizarding parents who have no magic themselves.

Chapter 3 will present a study concerned with the effect of reading *Harry Potter* on children and young adults. It will determine whether this paper's thesis is valid.

Chapter 4 deals with selected theories on reader identification. It will examine which factors influence which character the reader identifies with and whether this kind of identification has a long-term effect on the reader.

1. Discrimination: The fear of the Other?

Many reasons for discriminating behaviour lie in prejudice, which again is "conceptualized as an attitude that […] has a cognitive component (e.g., beliefs about a target group), an affective component (e.g., dislike), and a conative component (e.g., a behavioral predisposition to behave negatively toward the target group)" (Dovidio et al., *Prejudice* 2010, 5). So for people to develop discriminating behaviour, they first need to be in disfavour of a certain group of people, and then act on their feelings. These actions are generally seen as "inappropriate and potentially unfair treatment of individuals due to group membership" (ibid., 8), which does not necessarily have to be overtly negative behaviour, but can also result in more subtle actions like denial of positive reactions (cf. ibid. 8f).

Discriminating attitude can be evoked through a range of different feelings and causes. People who consider themselves the norm, or the ingroup, might experience milder feelings like dislike for people who deviate from that norm, the outgroup. An action against such would probably be equally moderate, like avoidance. Stronger hostility towards an outgroup could be caused if they received what the ingroup saw as unjust benefits. A probable reaction to that might be equally stronger, leading the discriminators to actively engage in reducing the outgroup's benefits. If the ingroup even felt threatened, this could invoke true hostile behaviour. Thus, discriminatory acts are highly influenced by the degree of danger the ingroup feels. (cf. ibid., 9).

Discriminatory behaviour may stem from only a single individual or from a group of people. However, it is also possible for higher agencies to display disfavour towards members of a certain group of people. This institutional discrimination "refers to the existence of institutional policies (e.g., poll taxes, immigration policies) that unfairly restrict the opportunities of particular groups of people" (ibid., 10). Institutional discrimination may be facilitated by the support of individuals, but it does not depend on it. In fact, often individuals do not recognise certain laws or policies as institutional discrimination. Either they are not challenged as unjustified because they are perceived as right since it is the law, or people might not question them, because those laws have a long tradition and are therefore considered normal and the way things have always been (cf. ibid. 10f).

Generally, discriminating behaviour is supposed to protect the status of the ingroup against a deviating outgroup, whether the perceived danger derives from the outgroup itself or another authority. The status marker used for unfair treatment is by no means invariable. People can find undesirable characteristics in many different areas, like religion or age (cf. Levin 2002, 228). In the following subchapters, I will introduce the markers of race in general, being black in particular and, lastly, disability and illness. I will highlight why members of these groups are being stigmatised and how actions against them are expressed.

1.1 Racism: Culture as marker for difference

The term 'race' was first used in the 16th century to differentiate between families and lineages (cf. Rattansi 2007, 23). The notion received a connotation more similar to our idea today in the 18th century. Swedish naturalist Carl Linnaeus divided humanity into four different races according to their origin, appearance and temperament, all of which were interconnected according to Linnaeus (cf. ibid., 25). In the 19th century, Robert Knox and Arthur de Gobineau further developed this idea. They, too, attributed specific markers, like skin colour or distinct features in their appearance, and, moreover, moral traits to certain races. Furthermore, they claimed that there was an innate hierarchy to races based on talent and beauty, with white people at the top and black people at the bottom (cf. ibid., 31). Today, the idea of races based on biological differences is less supported. Instead, the notion of being an ethnic Other is grounded on territorial belonging combined with different cultures. However, skin colour and culture are still strongly intertwined (cf. ibid., 97f), and although it is widely seen as a taboo to judge people based on their nationality or culture today, many still draw upon these differences in arguments (cf. ibid., 100).

Dovidio et al. (*Racism* 2010, 312) claim that racism has three defining elements. Firstly, they mention "distinguishing race-based characteristics that are common to their members" and, secondly, that these "perceived inherent racial characteristics of another group make it inferior to one's own group". They add a third aspect to that; a social power that enables people with a racist mindset to act on their negative attitude to either create disadvantages for other groups or advantages exclusively available for their own group. Nevertheless, according to Ottomeyer (2011, 170) it is already indicative of racism to express this mindset with pejorative or hateful utterances towards people of a different skin colour or culture.

However, not every race is equally discriminated. Often, there is a certain hierarchy with people of one colour being more accepted than another group, particularly when the colour is more similar to one's own (cf. Knapp 2008, 14). Yet many support the idea that different races should not mix and that races should keep their blood pure (cf. ibid., 20).

Racism had its latest climax in the mid-20th century, when Nazis singled out "Jews [as a] distinct race [which] posed a threat to the Aryan race to which authentic Germans supposedly belonged" (Rattansi, 2007, 4). Similar to the general idea of racism, Nazis in Germany distinguished between different grades of being Jewish. A person had to have at least three Jewish grandparents to be seen as a Jew. If they had only one or even two, it was possible for them to be regarded as German citizens and they were even allowed to fight in the German forces during the Second World War (cf. ibid., 6) as long as they "did not practise Judaism or marry Jews or other part-Jews" (ibid., 6). This also reflects the idea of keeping the blood of your race pure.

Although the idea of naturally inferior races based on biological differences has become a taboo after the Second World War, racism is far from extinct. In fact, since the term race is so closely linked to the genetic differences, we are not supposed to differentiate between races any more, but more between different cultures. However, this just seems like a way to talk around the actual problem (cf. ibid., 7f). While the constitution promises equal rights to people regardless of their nativity, skin colour or religion, there are still those who use exactly these distinctions to claim that there are better or inferior classes of people (cf. Knapp 2008, 22).

Expression of racism today is quite variable, with some people merely speaking out against different cultures and others taking more drastic actions. Different studies throughout Europe show partially strong tendencies against other cultures. Statements in these studies ranged from the conviction that foreigners should only marry people from their own countries – still reflecting the idea of keeping the blood pure – to the request that foreigners' rights should be restricted (cf. Ottomeyer 2011, 172f). However, we also experience frequent attacks against foreigners or refugee hostels (cf. Knapp 2008, 23).

These xenophobic attitudes are often a result of somebody's upbringing and passed on by the parents. However, bad experiences with someone from a certain culture can also lead to generalising notions about the whole race (cf. ibid., 24).

Concluding, many notions of racism still persist in people's minds, albeit under a different pretext. Racism started with scientists pointing out alleged inherent differences between the races and claiming that there would be a natural hierarchy because of these distinctions. Although today it is clear that there is no such thing as natural inferiority because of biology, people still use differences between cultures to take actions against members of these groups.

1.2 Slavery: The (ongoing) oppression of blacks

Along with the ideas of different races in the 16th century, as seen above, slave trade developed around the same time, with the first record of a black slave in Britain dating from 1554 (cf. Howard 2009, 39). The slave trade kept growing until it reached its peak in the 18th century (cf. Carey 2003, 107), particularly through the extension of the British empire to the New World (cf. Howard 2009, 39).

The slave trade was supported by the idea that black people were inferior by nature. In the eighteenth century, both Immanuel Kant and David Hume claimed that there had never been a more sophisticated race than white people, and that black people were not only inferior but also generally had lower intelligence than white people (cf. Rattansi 2007, 27). In fact, Africans were not even seen as wholly human. The slave trade had been legitimised by the notion that Africans were rather a sub-human species (cf. ibid., 29), which is why they also were not seen as proper citizens. This classification even gave Courts the right to withhold the privileges and immunities of citizenship from black people (cf. Levin 2002, 229).

Over the centuries, the slave trade and the supposed inferiority of black people turned into something like a social norm, a "widely accepted 'fact' that [was] very seldom or never questioned – neither by the master class nor by the slave class" (Brown 2008, 88). Most people, oppressed and oppressor alike, had accepted the circumstances enough to not even question how they came to be in the first place. They had become so deeply ingrained over a long period of time that people held on to these ideas because it was just the way thing were (cf. ibid., 88). From time to time, there have been slaves who tried to escape their situation and bring the system down, but these efforts were quickly been to an end and the rebel was looked down upon even by other slaves (cf. ibid., 88f). Of course, there have also been severe punishments for those who tried to escape, which was another reason why most blacks simply accepted their fate. They feared the retaliation and were intimidated by their masters. Most were not willing to risk the relative safety in slavery for an uncertain outcome. While they were fed and had a place to live, it was unsure if a rebellion would succeed (cf. ibid., 100), and even if it did, some slaves even feared freedom, for then they would have been responsible for their own actions and had to take care of themselves (cf. Howard 2009, 42).

However, the wind changed in the years following the American Independence. The voices condemning the slave trade became louder and a public pressure campaign demanding to prohibit human trafficking gained extensive support. The campaign did not bring immediate success, but the ongoing fight against slavery led to the abolition of the British slave trade in 1807 (cf. Carey 2003, 107).

The question remains whether the past 200 years brought real equality for black people. As we have seen above, the constitution promises equal treatment no matter the skin colour. However, studies show that particularly black people in the United States seem to be rather at a disadvantage. In 2001, the income of black families in the US was only 62% of that of white people, unemployment of black men was twice as high, and black children are three times as likely as white children to grow up in officially defined poverty. African Americans are the most geographically separated group in the US and often live in groups in areas with low income. On the upside, 75% of African American children achieve a High School diploma, but only 14% earn a college degree. Also, the number of black people in prison is comparatively high. While the black population in the US makes up about 12%, 50% of all prisoners are black. The death penalty rate for black people is twice as high compared to white convicts (cf. Rattansi 2007, 140-143).

In conclusion, African people have been exploited for centuries. Because of their skin colour, they have been seen not only as inferior but also as less intelligent. These assumptions have been used to excuse selling black people as slaves. Although the slave trade has been abolished for over 200 years, black African citizens are still not fully equal to whites.

1.3 Ill and Disabled: A burden for society?

The studies on discrimination against the ill and disabled are by far not as extensive as those seen above, but they are no less important. Miller et al. call this kind of discrimination disabilism and define it as "discriminatory, oppressive or abusive behaviour arising from the belief that disabled people are inferior to others" (2004, 9). The expression of prejudiced thinking against ill and disabled people range from discriminatory utterances to actively aggressive behaviour.

Disabled people are generally seen as less qualified than healthy people. It is assumed that they could never express their full potential and are less capable of achieving the same goals as non-disabled people. Thus, they are treated more often than necessary as people in need of charity and special services. Many are pitied for their circumstances (cf. ibid., 11f).

The human rights network Disability Awareness in Action set up a database recording attacks against disabled people using law reports and newspaper articles. According to this database, 682 disabled people were killed because of their condition between 1990 and 2004. These acts not only include crimes committed out of fear or hatred, but also mercy killings (cf. ibid., 15). Thousands more suffered from degrading treatment including verbal, physical or sexual abuse (cf. ibid., 24).

Disabled people also have difficulties receiving the education or employment they desire. In 2003, of all people with no health issues who applied for admission to a university, about 8% received a place. However, only 0.5% of disabled people who applied were admitted (cf. ibid., 24). Additionally, unemployment among disabled people is twice as high compared to healthy people. One third of those who do work receive less payment than their co-workers with no health problems (cf. ibid., 23).

Ill and disabled people are handicapped even in their social lives. Many people think that they themselves are responsible for their circumstances and that they are inferior because of their illness (cf. Gipser 2012, 122). As a result, disabled people are excluded from social activities; some mothers even abort their pregnancy if the child might be born disabled (cf. ibid., 123).

Often, ill and disabled people are expected to live within the prejudiced expectations set for them by healthy people have against them, so they rarely have the chance to exceed these expectations. For example, mentally challenged people are expected to be childlike and backward in their development, so they cannot be trusted with more complex operations. Rather, they are put together with people with similar disabilities. Therefore, they tend to have little contact with non-disabled people and virtually no chance to disprove the prejudices (cf. ibid., 126).

All in all, people with illnesses or disabilities are either regarded with pity, or they are discriminated against, sometimes even attacked for their afflictions, and they have fewer chances to realise their full potential personally or professionally. Although there are organisations fighting for equal rights, there is still much to do, similar to the other forms of discrimination outlined above.

2 *Harry Potter* – A short introduction

The book series tells the story of the eponymous Harry Potter, who, when he turns eleven, learns that he is a wizard. From then on, he must not only learn what is necessary to pass the tests of Hogwarts, the wizarding school, but also unravel the mysteries of his past. The evil wizard Voldemort tried to kill him when Harry was just a baby, and now Harry has to fight him again to save the wizarding race from Voldemort's cruel plans to reign.

Authors can draw from a large pool of methods to influence the way readers perceive their works. The narrator is an important tool in story-telling. The narrator necessarily reveals his relation to the events and characters, but also the viewpoint from which the story is perceived, and with comments or judgements, he also gives his opinion about the text (cf. Farner 2014, 33). If the narrator is a third-person narrator, it is possible for him to have insight to the feelings and thoughts of other characters; he is then omniscient (cf. ibid., 139). It is also useful to distinguish between covertness and overtness. If the reader receives information about the narrator himself, how he writes or tells the story, the narrator is overt, while complete lack of any hints about the narrator makes him covert (cf. ibid., 140). If the narrator is absent from the events we refer to him as heterodiegetic (cf. ibid., 206). Another important aspect is focalisation. The narrator has the option to focus on one or more characters to tell the story. He also can choose whether he tells the feelings and thoughts of those characters; the narrator then chooses internal focalisation (cf. ibid., 235). Moreover, there is the question of stability when it comes to focalisation. If the narrator chooses to follow mostly one character, his focalisation is constant, whereas switching between more characters leads to variable focalisation (cf. ibid., 239).

The choice of the narrator can serve different aims. Particularly if the narrator uses internal focalisation, it may lead to a closer understanding of that character and therefore might encourage identification with this character, as the reader is part of their world and feelings (cf. ibid., 256f).

Rowling's story features a heterodiegetic, omniscient narrator. He is a third-person narrator who is not part of the events taking place, yet has deep insights into the thoughts and feelings of the characters. However, the narrator mostly focuses on Harry, to tell the story from his point of view. There are very few chapters which focus on different characters. Nevertheless, these chapters are notably different from the rest.

While the Harry chapters make use of internal focalisation and give a lot of insight to his thoughts and feelings, the other chapters rather give only the facts with little evidence to the characters' emotions. While these chapters give crucial information which would not have been available if the narrator focused on Harry exclusively, the reader is apparently supposed to identify more with Harry.

2.1 The importance of blood-status: Are magical children of non-magical parents inferior witches and wizards?

In order to exemplify racism in her books, Rowling could have gone the direct route, as she has characters of many different cultures in her books. However, these characters are only very minor characters whom the reader gets to know very little about (cf. Ostry 93f). Rather, she creates a different way to deal with racism, the blood-status of her characters concerning their wizarding ancestry.

Most witches and wizards are born to equally magical parents. They are known as pure-bloods. It is also quite common to be born with magical powers if only one parent is a witch or wizard. Children of this ancestry are called half-bloods. However, although it is rare, it is possible that a witch or wizard is born to ordinary parents without any magic. Since people without magic are called Muggles, their magical children are known as Muggle-born. For some wizarding families, Rowling came up with the idea that pure-bloods or at least half-bloods are better wizards and witches than those born to Muggles. Often, these people descend from mighty aristocratic families, for it is easier for those with power to actively oppress others (cf. Flotmann 2013, 337), as we have already seen above.

This way of dealing with racism may be a politically correct way to do this. By using her characters' degree of wizard ancestry, "[it] is not Black- or Asian-British people who suffer because of their skin-colour but all people, black or white who do not have the 'right blood'" (ibid. 341). So in this way, people are not discriminated because of their skin colour, but all people from different cultures in our world are being treated the same.

Still, the group of Muggle-borns has to deal with several problems, the likes of which ethnic minorities in England and many other places must face today. They are ridiculed, verbally and physically attacked and later even persecuted, which is most clearly shown with one of the main characters, Hermione, who is a Muggle-born (cf. ibid. 336).

As it is with discriminative thinking in our world, the characters in *Harry Potter* seem to be very much influenced by their parents very much. Someone like Draco Malfoy, who grew up in a household that supports the idea that pure-bloods are superior, shows strong tendencies of the same discriminative thinking towards characters like Hermione, while Ron grew up with a father who is fascinated by Muggles and has a general reputation as a Muggle friend (cf. ibid. 338f), and Ron behaves accordingly.

Sometimes, Muggle-borns exceed pure-bloods in terms of magical skills. We see this very often with Hermione, whom Rowling depicts as one of the best in her class and apparently a much better witch than some of her pure-blood classmates. Pure-bloods might feel threatened by that fact. They do not understand how children from Muggles come to possess magical abilities in the first place, much less how such children can be better than theirs, and they fear they might lose the status pure-bloods have held for centuries (cf. ibid. 339). Also, they expect Muggle-borns to behave according to their status, that is, according to pure-bloods, Muggle-borns should rather be ashamed of their non-magical descent and not try to become something they are not supposed to be (cf. Brown 2008, 173).

While Rowling's discrimination of Muggle-borns shows many similarities to racism in general, it is also very reminiscent of the persecution of the Jews in particular (cf. Patient, Street 2009, 202). Voldemort's obsession with a pure race is reminiscent of Hitler, just like the fact that both were not part of the group they glorified. While Hitler was not the image of the pure Aryan race, Voldemort is not a pure-blood as his father was a Muggle (cf. Flotmann 2013, 339). In Nazi-Germany, Hitler took control of the Reichstag, founded a personal police force, and controlled the media, economy and education. Dolores Umbridge has no known affiliation with Voldemort, but she is an avid supporter of the pure-blood ideology. She is the *"Head of Muggle-born Registration Commission"* (Rowling 2007, 278) and her file on Mr Weasley reads: "*Blood Status: Pure-blood, but with unacceptable pro-Muggle leanings."* (ibid. 280). In *Harry Potter and the Order of the Phoenix*, Umbridge takes control over Hogwarts and shapes education to her liking. She also initiates her own squad to enforce her new rules (cf. Patient, Street 2009, 209), with Draco Malfoy in the lead, who shows a great likeness to Hitler's Aryan image with his pale face (Rowling 1997, 58) and silver-blond hair (Rowling 1999, 206).

Shortly after the First World War, people were still so shaken that they did not want to believe that Hitler was evil. Many rather thought he was a force of peace and stability. In *Harry Potter*, the reaction of the citizens of the wizarding world was similar. Many did not want to believe that Voldemort was back, so shortly after his first reign of terror, and ignored Dumbledore's warnings (cf. Patient, Street 2009, 214). Eventually, they were proven wrong when Voldemort seized power. One of his acts with the most impact was the Muggle Registration Act. Muggle-borns were forced to report to the Ministry of Magic. According to a newspaper article, the Ministry wanted to survey Muggle-borns to understand why they possessed magic as

> *[recent] research undertaken by the Department of Mysteries reveals that magic can only be passed from person to person when wizards reproduce. Where no proven wizarding ancestry exists, therefore, the so-called Muggle-born is likely to have obtained magical power by theft or force.* (Rowling 2007, 233)

While the idea of research to understand why Muggle-borns have magic does not necessarily sound evil in the first place, the idea of theft and force already implies that the Ministry holds a grudge against Muggle-borns. This becomes clearer as the article continues:

> *The Ministry is determined to root out such usurpers of magical power, and to this end has issued an invitation to every so-called Muggle-born to present themselves for interview by the newly appointed Muggle-born Registration Commission.* (ibid., 233)

The idea of rooting out these wizards sounds very much like Hitler's genocide of the Jews.

In addition, the Ministry hands out leaflets, to raise pure-bloods' awareness of the alleged dangers of Muggle-borns (cf. ibid., 277). In Nazi-Germany, Jews were similarly persecuted and imprisoned (cf. Patient, Street 2009, 225), including the distribution of anti-Jew pamphlets (cf. ibid. 219).

In the *Harry Potter* series, racism nearly exclusively emanates from characters the reader would deem evil. The first hints are dropped relatively early, when Draco Malfoy tries to convince Harry there are "some wizarding families [who] are much better than others" (Rowling 1997, 81), and that he wants to help him figure out who these families are. However, Harry simply replies that he "can tell who the wrong sort are for [himself]" (ibid., 81). Malfoy's hatred of Muggle-borns is shown clearly, when he calls Hermione a "filthy little Mudblood" (Rowling 1998, 86). According to Ron

> [it's] about the most insulting thing he could think of [...]. Mudblood's a really foul name for someone who was Muggle-born – you know, non-magic parents. [...] It's a disgusting thing to call someone [...] Dirty blood, see. Common blood. (ibid., 89)

When the Chamber of Secrets is about to open again, Draco remembers how the last time a Muggle-born was killed and hopes for a repetition of this event. He particularly enjoys the idea that it might be Hermione. (cf. ibid., 167). As already mentioned, Draco probably adopts much of his racist behaviour from his parents, as his father Lucius shows an even stronger hatred of Muggle-borns. Lucius even considered sending his son to a different wizarding school, Durmstrang. He is aware of Dumbledore's well-known appreciation of Muggle-borns, whereas the Headmaster of Durmstrang "doesn't admit that sort of riff-raff." (Rowling 2000, 147). Lucius even turns out to be a Death Eater, Voldemort's closest followers (cf. ibid., 564). Notably, both have been sorted into House Slytherin, whose founder practically started the thinking that pure-bloods are superior to Muggle-borns. Although the founders of the four houses of Hogwarts all shared the ideology of educating wizarding children

> [a] rift began to grow between Slytherin and the others. Slytherin wished to be more *selective* about the students admitted to Hogwarts. He believed that magical learning should be kept within all-magical families. He disliked taking students of Muggle parentage, believing them to be untrustworthy. (Rowling 1998, 114)

Harry very obviously does not follow this mindset. He repeatedly points out that Hermione is one of the best witches he knows, and when Malfoy teases Hermione that people are hunting Muggles and she should be careful, Harry retorts, "Hermione's a witch" (Rowling 2000, 110). At one point, Professor Slughorn contemplates how surprised he was to find out that Harry's mother was Muggle-born. She was such a good witch that Slughorn was convinced she must have been pure-blooded. He thinks it is rather funny how these things turn out sometimes. Harry, though, coldly refuses to agree with Slughorn's statements and emphasises again how Hermione is the best witch in his year (cf. Rowling 2005, 89).

Ron, too, rejects this idea equally, despite coming from a pure-blood family. He points out that all this pure-blood-thinking is madness (cf. Rowling 1998, 89). Then of course, his father works for Muggle rights in the Ministry, so he grew up with a different view on Muggles from the beginning. As much as Draco was born into a family who raised him to loathe Muggle-borns, Arthur Weasley is well-known for his fondness for Muggles. Although this apparently made him overlooked at promotions, because the Minister thinks Arthur would lack wizarding pride, he never wavers (cf. Rowling 2000, 617). It is likely that he raises his children to show equal respect for Muggles.

In conclusion, Rowling used the metaphor of wizarding blood-status to implement ideas about racism. Muggle-borns in the book world suffer from similar discriminations as people from other cultures in our society. In both cases, their ancestry and upbringing make people from these groups targets for degrading behaviour, as they are seen as inferior and less capable. However, it is mainly negative characters who display this sort of behaviour, above all Voldemort, who is the leading force behind the persecution of Muggle-borns. The positive characters, on the other hand, treat Muggle-borns as equals.

2.2 Unpaid work and abuse: House-elves in *Harry Potter*

House-elves in *Harry Potter* suffer an even worse fate than Muggle-borns. They are not even classified as human or human-like by wizards. When House-elf Winky is caught carrying a wand, it is declared that she broke the law because "[no] *non-human creature is permitted to carry or use a wand"* (Rowling 2000, 119). This could be a reason why it seems so easy for wizards to deny them basic human rights. These part-humans were only accepted in the wizarding community under terms the witches and wizards made. And to describe elves as something not entirely human gave them the excuse to exploit these beings. The same justifications were made during the times of the slave trade (cf. Brown 2008, 262). Elves are seen more like animals, inferior to the wizarding race, similar to how white people used to see Africans in the time of slave trading. House-elves are used for all kinds of labour in a wizarding household, from cooking to cleaning and any other kind of errand or task their master wishes of them. The elves have no other choice but to abide by their masters' orders, no matter if they want to carry them out or not. When Harry inherits the mastership to house-elf Kreacher, the elf complains long and loudly that he would never follow Harry's order. However, when Harry tells Kreacher to shut up, the elf has no other choice but to obey. As much as he tries to struggle against his new master's command, he cannot utter a single sound any more (cf. Rowling 2005, 67f). Allegedly, they also cannot even leave their masters' houses unless ordered to. However, if the elves are strong-minded enough, it does seem possible for them to rebel against these rules. They are tied to their masters' houses until they die or are set free, but as Harry remarks, it was possible for Dobby to leave the Malfoys' house to warn Harry. However, he still had to punish himself for that afterwards (cf. Rowling 2003, 556). Furthermore, he is being abused by the Malfoys for executing his tasks unsatisfactorily. Sometimes they simply demand that he hurt himself for no apparent reason, perhaps to remind him of his status (cf. Rowling 1998, 16).

In the wizarding world, it seems to be common understanding that house-elves like being enslaved. Particularly Ron repeatedly expresses this idea (cf. Rowling 2000, 198). There are very few masters who actually treat the elves with decency. After Harry frees Dobby from his enslavement to the Malfoys, Dobby tries to find paid work for two years, but is rejected by many families. Only Dumbledore is willing to employ him (cf. ibid., 328f). Dumbledore offered the elf ten Galleons a week with no work at weekends. However, this seemed to be too much for Dobby. He talks him down to one Galleon a week and only one day off a month. When Hermione complains that this is not enough, Dobby stresses that he does like freedom and payment, but he also does not want to ask for too much. After all, he still likes to work (cf. ibid., 330f). Is it possible that elves really prefer their enslavement? It is not entirely possible to answer this question with complete certainty. The novels give very little insight on how elf enslavement came to be. However, it is mentioned that elves have been enslaved for centuries (cf. ibid., 198), implying that it is not an inherent state of house-elves to be servants. There has to have been a time when elves were not enslaved. Also, it is implied that the elves' obedience is not inherent to their species either, but part of an enchantment (cf. ibid., 112). This enchantment in addition to the physical and psychical punishment is reminiscent of the abuse of Africans to bend them to their master's will. It only appears that elves in the books want to be enslaved, when in reality they have been subdued by various methods. However, this has been the way for centuries, and many wizards probably do not know how elf enslavement came to be. For them, it has always been this way and that is why they do not need to change it.

Another reason why house-elves may not want to be freed, is that they have been conditioned to see themselves the same way their masters see them. For centuries they have been told that they are lesser creatures and are born to serve. Generation after generation of elves were born into that kind of slavery and after being told that this is what they have to do, they started to believe it themselves (cf. Howard 2009, 44).

As already mentioned, there are many different ways to treat elves and Rowling tries to exemplify several of them. The Malfoys are the obviously negative characters here. They threaten and even abuse their house-elf, Dobby. Even after he has been freed, he still cannot talk badly about them without punishing himself. This treatment seems to be etched too deeply into his mind, so that Dobby cannot shake it off even years after no longer having to follow his former masters. After Dobby has been freed from the Malfoys, he wants to tell Harry that they are evil wizards. After some struggling, he is capable of saying the words, but immediately after that, he physically punishes himself (cf. Rowling 2000, 332). But physical abuse is not the only way to treat a house-elf poorly. In *Goblet of Fire*, the house-elf Winky is introduced. She is supposed to save seats for her master at the highest point of a stadium. Her master does not care that she is afraid of heights (cf. ibid., 90). African American slaves have equally been subdued by using physical and psychological violence (cf. Brown 2008, 93).

Voldemort himself also did not treat elves as equals. He misused his elf to test the magical defences around one of his Horcruxes, making the elf drink enchanted water which caused terrifying hallucinations and excruciating pain. Voldemort made use of what he thought of as a disposable creature to test his defences and then left the elf to die (cf. Rowling 2007, 217). At the time of the British slave trade, many slaves were equally sacrificed. During the voyage through the Middle Passage, countless slaves were thrown overboard, if they were sick, for instance, to ensure the rest of the passage (cf. Howard 2009, 38f).

Ron as someone who keeps defending Hermione and Muggle-borns in general, would rather be expected to be on the side of the good here as well. However, we have already seen that he is strongly under the impression that elves want to be enslaved and he sees nothing wrong with this. Ron is a typical example of someone who grew up with a certain set of beliefs he sees no need to challenge. For him, elves have always been enslaved and this is the status quo for him. This notion is supported by the law, as elves are not humans legally, so Ron does not see a reason to question what always has been. He does not necessarily treat elves badly, but this kind of ignorance is equally dangerous, as it prolongs the elves' enslavement unopposed (cf. Brown 2008, 113).

However, Ron's attitude towards the elves does improve slightly in the end. During the last battle of Hogwarts, he is the only one to think of evacuating the elves from the castle. He is immediately rewarded with Hermione kissing him for the first time (cf. Rowling 2007, 686).

Dumbledore shows much more kindness towards elves. Although most elves do not receive payment for working at Hogwarts, their treatment there seems tremendously better than in other wizarding households. Ron's brothers Fred and George repeatedly visit the kitchens and say the elves are happy and think they have "the best job in the world" (Rowling 2000, 211). As mentioned above, Dumbledore is also the only person who is willing to employ Dobby and actually pay him for his work.

However, the only person who wants to take action against the unfair treatment of the elves is Hermione. She is outraged when she learns about the elves' enslavement and is not shy to call it by that name exactly (cf. ibid., 162). She starts a campaign called "Society for the Promotion of Elfish Welfare" The short term aims

> are to secure house-elves fair wages and working conditions. [The] long term aims include changing the law about non-wand-use, and trying to get an elf into the Department for the Regulation and Control of Magical Creatures, because they're shockingly under-represented (ibid, 198)

Unfortunately she overstates her case by hiding pieces of clothing for the elves to find and therefore freeing them involuntarily (cf. Rowling 2003, 425).

In brief, house-elves are a clear metaphor for slavery. The elves are unpaid servants who have to follow their masters' commands and suffer severe punishments if they do not obey. The elves have very likely been subdued into submission over long periods of physical and psychological chastisement, similar to Africans during the slave trade. This has gone on for so long that it is seen as normal by most wizarding families. Again, the negative characters show strong discriminating tendencies towards house-elves. The positive characters are very biased though. Here it is important to make a distinction between those who grew up in the wizarding world like Ron, and those from the Muggle world like Hermione. While Ron grew up with the belief that elves are born to be servants, Hermione has a more differentiated view on this matter. However, in the end, even Ron comes to realise that the elves cannot be treated like simple property.

2.3 Non-magical children and Werewolves in the wizarding world

Disability issues in *Harry Potter* are not concerned with race or blood status. They derive from physical impairment which people are born with or have acquired through personal misfortune. Their lower status is not inherent, but made by the society. If the magical community had a different view on them, they would fare better in the world instead of being stigmatised and excluded (cf. Brown 2008, 120).

As seen above, being pure-blooded is depicted as something very important to several wizarding families. However, that alone is not always enough. Being magical is equally important. It seems that children who have witches and wizards as parents are usually magical themselves, but very rarely are they born without any powers. These children are called Squibs (cf. Rowling 1998, 110f). Squibs are treated poorly because they do not count as magical since they lack the ability to do magic, therefore they are an embarrassment for their families (cf. Brown 2008, 123). The term Squib itself is already derogative and shows wizards' attitude towards non-magical children. Parents seem to be ashamed of having Squibs in their families, often they are deported to the Muggle world. Ron's aunt Muriel elaborates how often Squib children were being kept a secret and

> usually shipped off to Muggle schools and encouraged to integrate into the Muggle community ... much kinder than trying to find them a place in the wizarding world, where they must always be second class (Rowling 2007, 174f)

This sounds very similar to how people treat disabled children in our world. Unfortunately, almost everyone seems to see Squibs as something to be ashamed of, even good families like the rest of the Weasley's. Ron's mother has a cousin who works in the Muggle world and is therefore assumed to be a Squib, but the family never talks about this cousin (cf. ibid., 74f). It is ocnce again only Dumbledore who treats them better than others do, as he gives work to a known Squib, Argus Filch (cf. Rowling 1998, 109). However, his employment is only as a caretaker, so it is questionable whether even Dumbledore sees him as suited for more complex tasks.

Werewolves are a similar matter, if not at first sight. While Squibs are a metaphor for disabled people, werewolves represent the ill. In contrast to Squibs, werewolves pose an actual physical threat, at least during their transformation and because they could pass on their condition. Although it is possible for them to control their instincts while in wolf form, it is still an excuse for the wizarding world to treat them badly (cf. Brown 2008, 123). For instance, werewolves are institutionally discriminated against since it is decreed that they shall not be employed. Umbridge "drafted a bit of anti-werewolf legislation two years ago that makes it almost impossible for [werewolves] to get a job" (Rowling 2003, 336). Yet again it is Dumbledore who defies this rule. He employs Remus Lupin as a teacher at Hogwarts. Ron is quite surprised that he did so and Lupin admits that Dumbledore had a hard time convincing some of the teachers (cf. Rowling 1999, 254). However, in the end it becomes common knowledge that Lupin is a werewolf and he is afraid of the parents' reactions toward his condition. To avoid trouble for Dumbledore, Lupin resigns from his teaching position (cf. ibid., 309).

Harry, Ron and Hermione seem to be biased when it comes to werewolves as well. At first it seems that they are heavily prejudiced. When they are under the understanding that Lupin works together with the man responsible for Harry's parents' deaths, they repeatedly use the term werewolf in a derogative way. For instance, Hermione warns Harry not to trust Lupin because he is a werewolf (cf. ibid., 253). However, they apparently do not have something against werewolves in general, but more against Lupin as long as they believe he is evil. Once they learn that everything has been a misunderstanding and Lupin is really on their side, he becomes one the most trusted friends to the group although he is a werewolf.

Discrimination of ill and disabled in *Harry Potter* is represented by prejudiced behaviour against non-magical children, Squibs, and werewolves. While Squibs have a difficult standing because of their lack of magic and are therefore mostly sent to work in the Muggle world, werewolves are legally discriminated against as there are decrees that prohibit them from being employed. Similar to the house-elf issue, even the good characters are rather prejudiced here. Ron's family prefers not to talk about their Squib relative, and his aunt points out how Squibs used to be sent to live with Muggles. Harry's, Ron's and Hermione's prejudiced attitude towards Lupin, the first werewolf they meet, however, seems to have little to do with his condition, but more with them thinking he is evil. They do use the term werewolf as an insult when they talk to him, but once they realise Lupin is a good person, they do not care if he is a werewolf any more.

As shown above, Rowling created many metaphors for people from stigmatised groups and the troubles they have in society. However, she does not simply state that treating an outgroup poorly is undesirable behaviour, but rather displays that by her characters' attitudes. The following chapter will present a study, analysing whether all these different ways of dealing with discrimination in *Harry Potter* may have an influence on the reader concerning their own view on prejudiced behaviour.

3 *"The greatest magic of* **Harry Potter"**

In 2014, Vezzali et al. published the methods and results of their study *The greatest magic of* Harry Potter*: Reducing Prejudice* concerning the effect of reading *Harry Potter* on prejudiced thinking. The purpose of the study was "to examine whether reading the novels of Harry Potter improves attitudes toward stigmatized groups" (Vezzali et al. 2014, 4). In three studies Vezzali et al. tested readers from various ages, from children to young adults to older adults. They tried to figure out whether the readers were influenced when they identified with the good or evil characters. In contrast to this paper, Vezzali et al. only expected participants to be positively influenced as long as they identified with Harry or showed a lack of identification with Voldemort (cf. ibid., 4).

The first study was conducted with elementary school children. In the first phase of the study, the children had to fill out questionnaires to determine whether they showed prejudiced behaviour. The participants were then split into two groups; group 1 read passages from *Harry Potter* that were related to the hypothesis, while group 2 read non-related excerpts. Both groups discussed the passages with a research assistant (cf. ibid., 4). Subsequent questionnaires and their analyses showed that reading and discussing prejudice-related excerpts improved attitudes towards immigrants when children identified with Harry Potter. Participants who showed a more negative attitude towards outgroups showed more identification with Voldemort, but this had no further effect on the second questionnaire (cf. ibid., 6).

The second study targeted the age group of high school students. They were tested for their attitude towards homosexuals. Here is was tested whether people who have already read the books show a better attitude towards the stigmatised group (cf. ibid., 6). The results were in line with the first study. Reading read the books and identifying with Harry Potter had a positive influence on behaviour and attitude towards homosexuals. Identifying with Voldemort does not seem to have any effect (cf. ibid., 8).

The last study tested the attitude of undergraduate students towards refugees. Again, this group had already read the *Harry Potter* books prior to the study (cf. ibid., 8). The results showed that readers who identified less with Voldemort had better attitudes toward refugees. However the perspective of Harry in the books did not seem to have an effect on that, maybe because the participants were too old to identify with such a young character (cf. ibid., 10).

In conclusion, the results from all studies showed that people who read *Harry Potter* displayed improved attitudes towards stigmatised groups as long as they identified with the positive characters or showed a lack of identification with the negative characters. However, in the first study, both aspects were equally important. Participants who identified with both Harry and Voldemort to some degree, showed inconclusive results (cf. ibid., 11).

Particularly for the first group with elementary children it was necessary to discuss the texts that were read. For children who read on their own, the story might have been too complex to filter out the message and meaning of what they had read. An educator can guide the readers to the importance of what they have read. Older children and young adults may be matured enough, so that the reading of this kind of book alone can be sufficient to improve their attitudes (cf. ibid., 13).

The subsequent chapter will introduce some theories about reader identification to explore how and why readers get involved with fictional characters in such a compassionate way.

4 Reader identification

In order to understand why readers would adopt a fictional character's attitude to some degree it is important to understand how messages are conveyed and how the reader identifies with the characters. Following, I will give an overview of the most well-established theories concerning this matter.

The school of Declinists believes that the moral of a story is fully transported to the reader. When children read a story of virtue they see that the deeds of the hero are good and preferable and will adopt this behaviour. Therefore, every child seems to see the same virtues in the story (cf. Narvaez 2002, 156). However, Narvaez argues that children import their own experiences while reading a story. Depending on what kind of experiences they made prior to reading something, these experiences can influence how they react to reading the story. They acquire a different understanding of a text because they integrate different information gained by individual experiences into the story (cf. ibid., 157). This way, a text can be distorted in two or more different ways depending on the experience the reader has made prior to reading the text (cf. ibid., 159). It becomes particularly problematic if readers come across a story with an unfamiliar theme, a theme they have no experience with, as they then tend to misinterpret the theme and state that the story is about something else, something they did have experience with (cf. ibid., 163f). Therefore, it should be noted that different readers may get different messages from a text depending on their backgrounds, and they might not get the message the author originally wanted to convey. Particularly moral themes require more sophisticated reading skills and mental development to be understood by the reader (cf. ibid., 169).

According to Cohen (2001),

"identification is defined not as an attitude, an emotion, or perception but, rather, as a process that consists of increasing loss of self-awareness and its temporary replacement with heightened emotional and cognitive connections with a character." (251)

He also states that this kind of identification is different from the identification we experience in real life. In contrast to the people we identify with in real life, such as social groups or leaders, the identification with fictional characters is intended. The author provides textual features that invite the reader to identify with the characters in order to interact with and enjoy the text in a more intense way. Unlike with real people, the reader comes across the characters in carefully constructed scenarios. Cohen also points out that this sort of identification is rather an internalisation of someone else's point of view than projecting the readers' own views on the character (cf. ibid., 251f).

The process of identification may be set in motion by different factors. Some of the most common are that the reader finds similarities between himself and the character, or that he grows particularly fond of a character for reasons other than alikeness. This may not only lead to attachment but rather a merging between character and reader. For a while, the reader shares similar goals in the narrative and adopts the character's personality (cf. ibid., 252).

Identification might produce mixed or even contrary feelings within the reader. It may bring the reader to like a character even more and sometimes even imitate their behaviour. However, it can also lead to negative feelings. These contradicting feelings arise particularly when it comes to evil characters. On the one hand, the reader could feel sympathy or show understanding for them. On the other hand, strong identification may induce guilt or shame (cf. ibid., 252).

Cohen sees identification as a useful "persuasion tactic because it can overcome the natural tendency to limit one's thoughts and feelings to a single perspective" (ibid. 260). It not only gives the reader the opportunity to gain a view on other perspectives, but more importantly a way of understanding them that may lead to a change in attitude in the reader (cf. ibid., 260).

Konijn and Hoorn (2005) also state that similarity is one of the factors for identification, but that there are also many others (cf. 108). According to them, it is also important that most characters produce mixed feelings. Fictional characters who show good and bad features, create inner conflicts and cause suspense. Therefore, they are seen as more interesting (cf. ibid., 100), which encourages identification.

But even characters with mostly bad features can evoke positive feelings in the reader. If the evil character is described as particularly ugly, for example, the reader might feel sympathy or pity for him (cf. ibid., 110). In fact, evil characters with bad looks cause more positive feelings than handsome evil characters. This might be because beautiful people are already perceived as privileged and should have other ways to get what they want, while ugly characters are seen as people who have no other chance than to become evil (cf. ibid., 133).

Mental processes like identification can be controlled or automatic. Controlled processes are started intentionally, the person is aware of the process, and the outcome manifests slowly. Automatic processes start without intention, the person is not aware, and the process works quickly (cf. Harold 2005, 175). There are explanations for both processes. Identification as a controlled process states that fiction does not affect the reader on its own. It gives the reader the opportunity to reflect on their own beliefs, make or refine judgements or reconsider the readers' already existing moral mindsets. However, as identification is perceived as a controlled process, this only happens when the reader chooses to do so (cf. ibid., 177). Therefore, the reader is actively engaged in the possible alteration of their beliefs. It would seem unlikely that they would let evil characters affect their morale (cf. ibid., 178).

It appears much more interesting to view identification as an automatic process. The theory is that if readers focus on a character for a longer period of time, they start imagining what they would do if they were the character, and if they do that for a long time, the character's desires infect the readers' desires. Since this is seen as an automatic process, this happens without the readers' influence (cf. ibid., 180). Studies show that readers' attitudes change after reading fiction. However, most readers mainly adopt feelings and beliefs coming from the main character. This would imply that readers could also take on behaviour from evil characters if they were the main character or at least prominently presented (cf. ibid., 181f). There is still a difference between alignment and allegiance. Through excessive portrayal of evil characters, the readers are practically forced to concern themselves with their behaviour, but they cannot be forced to show allegiance for that character. However, alignment can lead to allegiance over a long period of time, particularly when the reader finds similarities to the character (cf. ibid., 182). As this process of contagion is automated, the readers might not realise that they adopt good or bad character traits, even if they are morally harmful (cf. ibid., 183).

These theories are in line with the study on *Harry Potter*. Whether the reader was strongly affected by the story depended on similarities or dissimilarities. Young adults who exhibit less prejudiced behaviour described that they identified with Harry, while adult readers pointed out that there was a strong lack of identification with Voldemort.

Particularly interesting is of course the result of the first phase of the study. Again, readers who claimed to identify with Harry showed an improvement in their behaviour. The results of those who showed allegiance to Voldemort were rather inconclusive. According to the theories of reader identification, it might be important that the reader already shares some opinions of the character, maybe even subconsciously, or at least finds some other similarities with them, as seen above with the identification with Harry or lack of identification with Voldemort. The younger readers identify more with Harry, probably partly because they are of a similar age, while the older readers might find it difficult because of the age difference. They rather compare themselves with Voldemort. The result, though, is the same, no matter if the reader identifies with the good characters or disidentifies with the bad characters. Both groups of readers would probably improve their thinking concerning discriminative thinking. However, if the reader rather identifies with the negative characters, for whatever reason, they are less likely to show these results. As the study on *Harry Potter* has shown, readers identifying with Voldemort showed inconclusive results. It is to be clarified why their behaviour did not worsen. One possible explanation might be that the *Harry Potter* series does not give enough insight into Voldemort's motives. As the theories have shown, it seems important to spend a long time with a character to adopt his views, and although Voldemort is, of course, an important character as well, the introduction to chapter 2 has shown that most of the books are written with the focus on Harry, and the few chapters which tell the story from another point of view are written in a quite distanced fashion. Rowling apparently wants the readers to identify with Harry, so the people who do identify with Voldemort have very few possibilities to take on his views.

One last important aspect to review is the dichotomy of some characters. As seen above, many of the good characters do show some prejudiced tendencies towards some outgroups, but not to others. If generally well-disposed readers tend to identify with good characters, how can it be that they seem to identify with characters with such contrasting behaviour? As the theories above have shown, it is particularly such characters that appeal most to the reader. They are not only the most credible characters because real life is not just black and white, but they are also most interesting in terms of dramaturgy. It is exactly these characters who make a story more suspenseful.

In conclusion, readers tend to identify with characters similar to themselves. Over time, they might even come to understand different characters, but these would have to be presented in an appealing enough way. Either way, long exposure to a (main) character can bring the reader to adapt their opinions. J.K. Rowling's *Harry Potter* series focuses mainly on Harry and by extension his closest friends and attachment figures. All of them are flawed characters, but basically good, with little to no prejudiced attitude. Readers who identify with them consequently show improved behaviour concerning discrimination. However, readers who identify with Voldemort are given too few opportunities to take on his opinions.

Conclusion

Discrimination has a very long history. For centuries, people have been judged on the basis of different skin colour, distinct physical features or their beliefs. It has been believed that people who look differently were naturally inferior. People belonging to an outgroup were assumed to be inherently less intelligent and therefore could be treated badly. Over time and with evolving science, these alleged biological markers lost their persuasiveness, but people replaced them with different markers, like culture. Even today, skin colour, belief, and culture lead people to be prejudiced. Discrimination ranges from demoting thinking, over active participation in attempts to reduce foreigners' rights, to actual physical attacks on members of outgroups.

Black people in particular still suffer from the aftermath of slavery. For hundreds of years they were sold and forced to work in their masters' houses and fields, often too scared or too much forced into submission to do something against their predicament. However, even after the abolition of slavery, black people are still often treated as inferior to white people. They earn less for the same work, more black people are unemployed and the penal system favours white people.

But race alone is not always a marker for being discriminated. Ill and disabled people have to live with many prejudices as well. Employers prefer healthy workers, other people pity them or do not know how to deal with them. Often, disabled people are put together in homes or groups with others who share their affliction, and therefore have little chance to convince society that they might be able to perform tasks like healthy people.

In order to take measures against these problems it is important to find various ways of changing people's minds. One of these ways might be through literature. Particularly for children it may be difficult to find a way to deal with this in a way that keeps them interested. If the issues of discrimination were wrapped in an intriguing story, this might be a way to make children, or adults, aware of the problems.

J.K. Rowling approaches different issues of discrimination in her *Harry Potter* series. She does not do so in a direct way, but implements metaphors so as not to stigmatise an actual group of her readership. Instead of showing discrimination against certain races and cultures, Rowling uses the blood status of her characters. Being of magical ancestry is of utmost importance to some wizarding families in the books. If wizards or witches do not have any magical parents, they are seen as inferior and less capable. After Voldemort's rise to power, these Muggle-borns are even persecuted and treated like criminals.

Although the issue of slavery is also not exemplified with the actual group of people who had to suffer from it in our world, this metaphor is much more obvious.

House-elves are servants of wizarding families. They have to follow their masters' every order, sometimes they are abused for disobedience, and their work is unpaid. The enslavement of elves goes on for so long that wizards do not even question this circumstance anymore, claiming that the elves even want to be enslaved. Only Hermione, who grew up in a Muggle household, sees the situation for what it is and tries to do something against it.

Non-magical children and werewolves represent the discrimination against the disabled and ill. These two groups from the books suffer from the same, mostly institutional discrimination as in our world. Many have troubles finding work, or are forced to live with equally afflicted people.

It is not only important that these topics are dealt with generally, but also in what way. In most cases the good characters are friendly towards stigmatised groups and treat them like equals, while the negative characters are often driving forces behind discriminatory acts. However, Rowling's world is not so simply black and white. Often, even good characters show tendencies of prejudice, though none of them are downright hostile.

Whether or not the intended messages of stories influences the reader in the intended way depends on different factors. One of the most important one is the identification with the characters. If readers are in touch with a character over a long period of time it seems that they do adopt some of the character's thinking, particularly, but not exclusively, if they identify with them. An often assumed theory is that readers identify with characters which share some similarities with themselves. This would mean that the reader might already share some of the character's views on certain issues – although similarities could also be shared events from the past, or simply appearance – but subconsciously. Identification with the character then amplifies the readers' opinions. The study on the possibility that *Harry Potter* might change the readers' thinking concerning prejudice seems to support these theories. As long as readers identified with Harry Potter or showed a lack of identification with Voldemort, they displayed a less prejudiced attitude towards stigmatised groups.

In conclusion, the representation of discrimination in *Harry Potter* has the potential to improve readers' attitudes towards outgroups, but only if they identify with the positive characters who display a positive view on stigmatised people.

Literature

Brown, Karen A. *Prejudice in Harry Potter's World*, College Station: Virtualbookworm.Com Publishing, 2008.

Carey, Brycchan. "Hermione and the House-Elves: The Literary and Historical Contexts of J.K. Rowling's Antislavery Campagne." In: *Reading Harry Potter – Critical Essays*, Giselle Liza Anatol (Publ.), Westport: Praeger, 2003. 103-115.

Cohen, Jonathan. "Defining Identification: A Theoretical Look at the Identification of Audiences With Media Characters." In: *Mass Communication and Society* 4.3, 2001. 245-264.

Dovidio, John F. et al. "Prejudice, Stereotyping and Discrimination: Theoretical and Empirical Overview." In: *The SAGE Handbook of Prejudice, Stereotyping and Discrimination*, John F. Dovidio et al. (Publ.), Los Angeles: Sage, 2010. 3-28.

Dovidio, John F. et al. "Racism." In: *The SAGE Handbook of Prejudice, Stereotyping and Discrimination*, John F. Dovidio et al. (Publ.), Los Angeles: Sage, 2010. 312-327.

Farner, Geir. *Literary Fiction – The Ways We Read Narrative Literature*, New York: Bloomsbury Academic, 2014.

Flotmann, Christina. *Ambiguity in "Star Wars" and "Harry Potter"*, Bielefeld: Transcript, 2013.

Gipser, Dietlinde. "Krank, alt, behindert – nutzlos oder kostbar für die Gesellschaft." In: *Vorurteile – Ursprünge, Formen, Bedeutung*, Sir Peter Ustinov Institut (Publ.), Berlin: de Gruyter, 2012. 113-145.

Harold, James. "Infected by Evil." In: *Philosophical Explorations: An International Journal for the Philosophy of Mind and Action* 8.2, 2005. 173-187.

Howard, Susan. "'Slaves No More': The Harry Potter Series as Postcolonial Slave Narrative." In: *Harry Potter's World Wide Influence*, Diana Patterson (Publ.), Newcastle: Cambridge Scholars, 2009, 35-47.

Knapp Anja. *Rassistische Tendenzen bei den Harry Potter Antagonisten?*, Saarbrücken: VDM, 2008.

Konijn, Elly A., and Johan F. Hoorn. "Some Like It Bad: Testing a Model for Perceiving and Experiencing Fictional Characters." In: *Media Psychology* 7.2, 2005. 107-144.

Levin, Brian. "From Slavery to Hate Crime Laws: The Emergence of Race and Status-Based Protection in American Criminal Law." In: *Journal of Social Issues* 58.2, 2002. 227-245.

Miller, Paul et al. *Disabilism*, London: Demos, 2004. pdf.
<file downloadable at: http://www.demos.co.uk/files/disablism.pdf>

Molle, Cheryl Anne. *Racial otherness and the Harry Potter series*, n.p. 2013. ebook.

Narvaez, Darcia. "Does Reading Moral Stories Build Character?" In: *Educational Psychology Review* 14.2, 2002. 155-171.

Ostry, Elaine. "Accepting Mudbloods: The Ambivalent Social Vision of J.K. Rowling's Fairy Tales." In: *Reading Harry Potter – Critical Essays*, Giselle Liza Anatol (Publ.), Westport: Praeger, 2003. 89-101.

Ottomeyer, Klaus. "Rassismus." In: *Vorurteile – Ursprünge, Formen, Bedeutung*, Sir Peter Ustinov Institut (Publ.), Berlin: de Gruyter, 2011. 169-204.

Patient, Aida, and Kori Street. "Holocaust History Amongst the Hallows – Understanding Evil in Harry Potter." In: In: *Harry Potter's World Wide Influence*, Diana Patterson (Publ.), Newcastle: Cambridge Scholars, 2009. 201-228.

Patterson, Diana. "Preface." In: *Harry Potter's World Wide Influence*, Diana Patterson (Publ.), Newcastle: Cambridge Scholars, 2009. vii-xii.

Rattansi, Ali. *Racism – A Very Short Introduction*, Oxford: Oxford University Press, 2007.

Rowling, Joanne K. *Harry Potter and the Philosopher's Stone*, London: Bloomsbury Publishing, 1997 (2001).

Rowling, Joanne K. *Harry Potter and the Chamber of Secrets*, London: Bloomsbury Publishing, 1998 (2002).

Rowling, Joanne K. *Harry Potter and the Prisoner of Azkaban*, London: Bloomsbury Publishing, 1999 (2004).

Rowling, Joanne K. *Harry Potter and the Goblet of Fire*, London: Bloomsbury Publishing, 2000 (2005).

Rowling, Joanne K. *Harry Potter and the Order of the Phoenix*, London: Bloomsbury Publishing, 2003 (2004).

Rowling, Joanne K. *Harry Potter and the Half-blood Prince*, London: Bloomsbury Publishing, 2005 (2006).

Rowling, Joanne K. *Harry Potter and the Deathly Hallows*, London: Bloomsbury Publishing, 2007 (2008).

TIME, *Because It's His Birthday: Harry Potter, By The Numbers*. July 31, 2013. <accessible at: http://entertainment.time.com/2013/07/31/because-its-his-birthday-harry-potter-by-the-numbers/>

Vezzali, Loris et al. "The greatest magic of *Harry Potter*: Reducing prejudice." In: *Journal of Applied Social Psychology*, published online 23 July, 2014. pdf.
<file downloadable at: http://onlinelibrary.wiley.com/doi/10.1111/jasp.12279/pdf>